SIMPL
IMPRO

*your
storage
space*

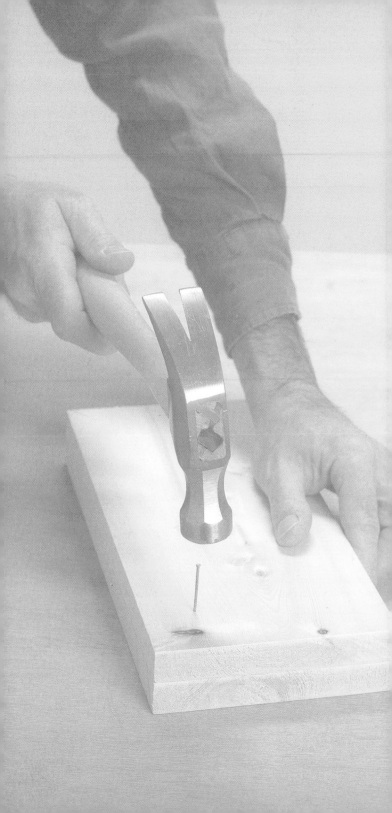

SIMPLE HOME
IMPROVEMENTS

your storage space

STEWART WALTON

MARSHALL PUBLISHING • LONDON

A Marshall Edition
Conceived, edited and designed by
Marshall Editions
The Orangery
161 New Bond Street
London W1Y 9PA

First published in the UK in 2000 by Marshall Publishing Ltd

ISBN: 1-84028-381-5

Originated in Singapore by Pica.
Printed and bound in China by Excel Printing.

Project Editor Ian Kearey

Designed by Paul Griffin

Photographer Alistair Hughes

Managing Editor Antonia Cunningham

Managing Art Editor Patrick Carpenter

Editorial Director Ellen Dupont

Art Director Dave Goodman

Editorial Coordinator Ros Highstead

Production Amanda Mackie

Indexer Jill Dormon

Front cover photography: **Colin Poole** Back cover: **Alistair Hughes**

Note

contents

Introduction   *6*

Chapter 1: Storage

Making a toy box   10

Makling a hall settle   18

Making a bookcase   28

Making a window seat   36

Making an accessory stand   46

Chapter 2: Shelving

Fitting an alcove shelf   56

Making a hall shelf   64

Making a shelf with coat rail   70

Chapter 3: Closets

Making a shoe rack   78

Making a wardrobe with loose cover   86

Fitting an alcove storage unit   94

Fitting louvre doors   102

Glossary   *110*

Index   *111*

introduction

For most of us, finding places to keep things neatly is a perennial problem – shoes, toys, books and magazines, to name a few objects, have a habit of spreading themselves everywhere. There are two practical ways to solve this: the first, throwing everything but the very bare essentials out and living a spartan, minimalist and rugged life, is achieved (or even desired) only by a small minority; the rest of us have to follow the second line, that of least resistance, and purchase or make storage solutions. A brief look in all but the most expensive stores will show that attractive designs don't always mean the best quality of materials or construction, so take pride in your work and make your own!

In this book, I designed the projects to be accessible to as wide a range of people as possible. In the introduction to each set of step-by-step photographs and text, the project is given a skill rating of Beginner, Intermediate, or Advanced. Of course in the wardrobe with loose fabric cover, to give just one example, someone with experience in woodworking, for whom cutting joints poses no problem, may find using a sewing machine a tough proposition, and the reverse will be true for a practiced tailor or seamstress.

The important thing is to look at all the stages of each project before you tackle it and, above all, take your time – the times given in the introductory section for the projects assume you have all the materials and tools to hand and can

work uninterruptedly until you have finished. The additional work needed to finish a project – treating wood, applying protection, painting and varnishing – are not included in the times, nor are drying times for glue, wood filler and finishes.

Note that the dimensions given in the Materials lists are for the finished size of each component as made for this book; you can adapt the projects to fit your own requirements, especially those made to fit a particular alcove or similar space. If you are planning to change the size radically, you may have to reconsider the width and depth you use for each component, both for strength and proportions.

When it comes to tools, the golden rule is that you get what you pay for. Inexpensive tools may seem a bargain, but their drawbacks can range from measuring inaccurately to falling apart while working – and for power tools, this can lead to injury or worse. Make a careful check on secondhand tools, and inspect the wiring in electrical tools.

Don't let these dire warnings put you off. If you follow the manufacturer's instructions, and wear protective clothing where necessary, you should not have a problem. Good tools do cost, so build up your tool kit as and when you can; and to save spending money on equipment that may only be used once or twice, most rental stores hire out large and small power tools by the day or weekend.

I hope you get enjoyment and a sense of having achieved something worthwhile out of these projects.

Stewart Walton

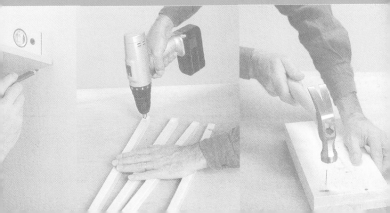

chapter 1
Storage

1. Making a toy box

2. Making a hall settle

3. Making a bookcase

4. Making a window seat

5. Making an accessory stand

making a
toy box

Children's toys seem to have a mind of their own, and spend much of their time not being where they should be – so a sturdy storage box is pretty essential. Even if you don't have children, the box can be used for keeping a variety of things in, and the casters mean you can take it from room to room as it is needed. You can paint cheerful, contrasting colours to brighten up or match a room, or think about more adventurous decorative techniques, such as stencilling or freehand painting.

Materials (all timber is MDF unless otherwise stated)

2 pieces 460 x 19 x 330 mm (18 x ¾ x 12⅞ in) • 1 piece 510 x 19 x 460 mm (20 x ¾ x 18 in) • 1 piece 510 x 19 x 380 mm (20 x ¾ x 15 in) • 1 piece 510 x 19 x 268 mm (20 x ¾ x 10½ in) • 1 piece 510 x 19 x 293 mm (20 x ¾ x 11½ in) • 1 piece softwood 510 x 16 x 32 mm (20 x ⅝ x 1¼ in) • 2 pieces softwood 268 x 16 x 32 mm (10½ x ⅝ x 1¼ in) • 38-mm (1½-in) no. 6 screws • 25-mm (1-in) no. 6 screws • 4 casters, 50 mm (2 in) top to bottom

Tools

Jigsaw or coping saw • Crosscut saw • Combination square • Straightedge • Power or bench plane • Screwdriver • Drill with 38-mm (1½ in), 25-mm (1-in) and countersink bits • Abrasive paper and cork or foam block • PVA glue • Wood putty

Skill level

Beginner/Intermediate

Time

2–3 hours

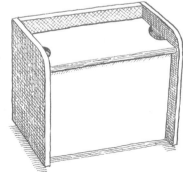

1 Cut the two sides to 460 x 330 mm (18 x 12⅞ in) from 19-mm (¾-in) MDF, and check the corners for square. Position a 150-mm (6-in) baking tin or plate so that it's touching the two front edges of the sides, and draw a curve around the top of the plate with a pencil.

2 Shade in the waste MDF and cut around the curve – a power jigsaw makes this task easy, otherwise you can use a coping saw. Check that both sides are identical, and sand to adjust if required.

Helpful hints

MDF produces a lot of possibly harmful dust when sawn, drilled or sanded. Wear a dust mask when working it, and use dust extractors if fitted to your power tools.

3 Cut the box lid to 510 x 293 mm (20 x 11½ in) from 19-mm (¾-in) MDF. Check that the corners are square, then use the plate or tin to trace the curves for the openings at each end – the holes should start 88 mm (3½ in) from the front edge and 75 mm (3 in) from the back. Shade the waste and cut with a power jigsaw or coping saw.

4 Clamp the lid in your workbench or vice, and plane and sand down the sides to produce a rounded finish. Cut the back to 510 x 460 mm (20 x 18 in) and the front to 510 x 380 mm (20 x 15 in) from 19-mm (¾-in) MDF.

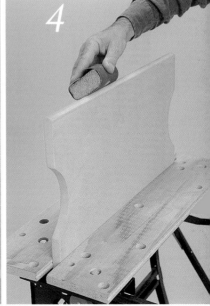

5 Mark out positional guides on the side panels for the positions of the back, front and base, using the actual pieces to mark out lines for an exact fit. The bottom of the base should finish 32 mm (1¼ in) above the bottom of the sides, back, and front, to allow turning room for the casters.

6 Cut the two base battens to 268 mm (10½ in) from 16 x 32 mm (⅝ x 1¼ in) softwood. Mark, drill and countersink three pilot holes in each batten, then place each in turn against one side with its top edge meeting the base line. Mark through the pilot holes with a bradawl, then screw in place using 38-mm (1½-in) no. 6 screws.

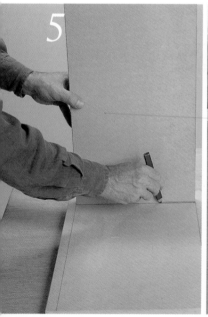

7 Lay the back and one side butted up together, with their bottom edges meeting exactly. Using a square and straightedge, draw a horizontal line from the top of the front position on the sides along the back. This is the lower edge of the lid batten. Cut the batten to 510 mm (20 in) from 16 x 32 mm (⅝ x 1¼ in) softwood. Drill and countersink three pilot holes, apply glue, and insert and drive in 25-mm (1-in) no. 6 screws.

8 Lay the back flat and hold one side vertically in position, checking for square. Mark and drill three equidistant screw holes along the side inside the marked lines. Drill pilot holes through the sides into the back and countersink them, then apply glue and drive in 38-mm (1½-in) no. 6 screws.

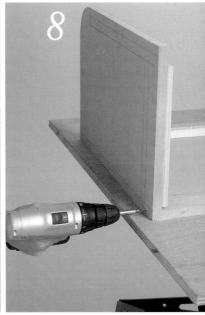

9 Position the base so it sits in place on top of the base battens. As for the sides, drill and countersink two equidistant pilot holes through the sides inside the marked lines, then apply glue and drive in 38-mm (1½-in) no.6 screws.

10 Hold the front position the same way as in steps 8 and 9. Drill and countersink two pilot holes through the sides and three along the front into the base, then apply glue and drive in 38-mm (1½-in) no. 6 screws.

11 Turn the box upside down and place each caster in position. To ensure that the wheels run freely, position them near the corners but far away from the sides, front and back. Mark the screw positions through the holes in the casters with a pencil, then bradawl the holes and drive in the screws firmly.

12 Using a filling knife, fill all the screw holes with wood filler. Allow it to dry and sand it smooth. Give the whole box and lid a final light sanding, wipe off, then paint using emulsion or semi-matt water-based paint. (You don't need to use primer on MDF.)

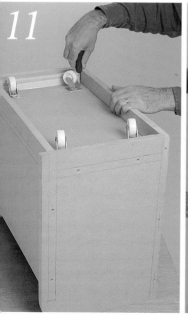

making a
hall settle

Settles with removable or hinge-opening lids or seats and storage room inside have been popular for centuries. They were originally made of long-lasting hardwood; resin-bonded MDF, as used in this project, is claimed to have the same stability. This settle uses only butt joints and is glued and screwed together. If you have a large hall or wall space, consider extending the width, but keep the simple symmetry of this version.

Materials (all timber is MDF unless otherwise stated)

1 piece 760 x 19 x 710 mm (30 x ¾ x 28 in) • 2 pieces 485 x 19 x 268 mm (19 x ¾ x 10½ in) • 1 piece 748 x 19 x 510 mm (29½ x ¾ x 20 in) • 1 piece 800 x 19 x 230 mm (31½ x ¾ x 9 in) • 1 piece 800 x 19 x 75 mm (31½ x ¾ x 3 in) • 1 piece 785 x 19 x 88 mm (31 x ¾ x 3½ in) • 1 piece 305 x 19 x 88 mm (12 x ¾ x 3½ in)• 1 piece 710 x 19 x 250 mm (28 x ¾ x 9¾ in) • 1 piece softwood 710 x 19 x 38 mm (28 x ¾ x 1½ in) • 3-mm (1½-in) no. 6 screws • 2 brass flush hinges 50 mm (2 in) long with brass screws

Tools

Crosscut saw or jigsaw • Combination square • Mitre saw • Straightedge • Bradawl • Pencil • Drill with pilot hole and countersink bits • Screwdriver • Abrasive paper and sanding block • Spirit level • PVA glue • Wood filler • Filling knife

Skill level

Intermediate

Time

3–4 hours

1 Cut the back to 760 mm (30 in) height and 710 mm (28 in) width. Mark the top edge, then measure 280 mm (11 in) from the top on each side and draw a line across the width. Mark 50 mm (2 in) along the top from the edges and along the drawn line, then join the marks with a vertical line. Shade in the waste and mark a diagonal line between marks made 25 mm (1 in) along the top and the vertical line.

2 Use a crosscut saw or jigsaw to cut out the waste MDF on each side, then cut along the diagonal lines to create bevels at the top. Sand the cut edges smooth with abrasive paper wrapped around a sanding block.

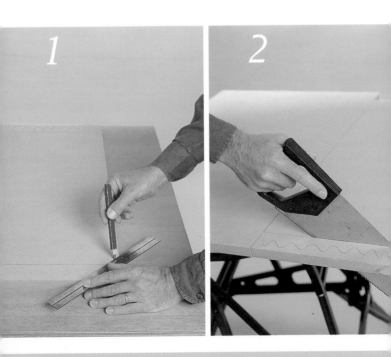

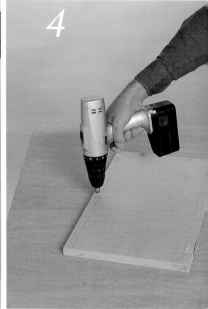

3 Cut a 19 x 38 mm (¾ x 1½ in) piece of softwood to
710 mm (28 in) and sand the ends. Drill and countersink three equidistant pilot holes through the batten
and position it with its upper edge meeting the line
across the back. Mark through the holes with a
bradawl, apply glue, and drive in 38-mm (1½-in) no.
6 screws.

4 Cut the two sides to 485 x 268 mm (19 x 10½ in).
Draw a line 19 mm (¾ in) inside each back and base
edge, and within this line mark, drill and countersink
three pilot holes for the back and two for the base.

Simple home improvements

5 Position one side to the back, with the top of the side level with the top of the batten and the rear edge of the back exactly meeting the edge of the side. Drill through the pilot holes into the side edge of the back, apply glue, then drive in 38-mm (1½-in) no. 6 screws, making sure the corner is square. Repeat for the other side.

6 Cut the base to 710 x 250 mm (28 x 9¾ in). Position it between the edge and drawn lines on the sides and drill pilot holes into the edges through the holes in the sides. Apply glue and drive in screws. Cut the front to 748 x 510 (29½ x 20 in) and draw a line 19 mm (¾ in) inside the side edges. Drill and countersink three pilot holes, then apply glue and screw to the sides.

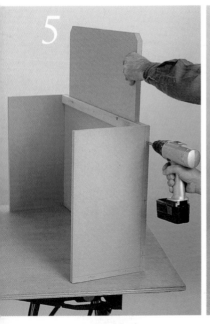

7 The movable lid and seat back are cut in one piece initially. Measure and mark a piece of MDF to 800 x 305 mm (31½ x 12 in), and cut it using a jigsaw or crosscut saw.

8 Lay the carcase on its back and position the lid/seat-back piece butting up to the sides and front; the MDF overhang at each side should be 25 mm (1 in). Mark where this piece meets the cut-out on the back and use a square to draw a line across it. Measure 19 mm (¾ in) along these lines, join them and cut out the waste to fit the back.

9 Position the carcase upright and fit the lid/seat-back piece in its place, butting up to the back firmly. Measure 75 mm (3 in) along the sides of the lid/seat-back from the back and use a straightedge to draw a line across the piece. Cut the piece with a jigsaw or fine-tooth crosscut saw, then smooth the cut edges.

10 Use a square to draw two lines across the shallow piece (the seat-back) at the start of the cut-outs. Close the flush hinges and place them with their centre on these marks, then butt up the lid with its sides meeting the seat-back sides exactly. Draw lines to meet the hinge ends across both pieces with a square.

11 Continue the lines onto the meeting edges of the seat-back and lid. Hold the seat-back on its rear edge, position the large part of the hinges to the lines, and mark and drill guide holes for the hinge screws. Drive in the screws, then hold the lid and seat pieces together and mark and drill guide holes in the lid and screw the hinges in place.

12 For the plinth side, cut one end of a length of 19 x 88 mm (¾ x 3½ in) square, hold it against the rear of one side, and mark the front edge of the carcase. Set a mitre saw to 45 degrees and cut a mitre with the mark at the inner edge; the total length is 305 mm (12 in). Repeat for the other side.

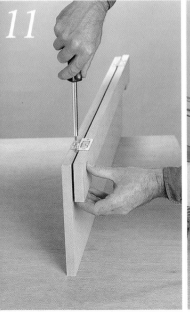

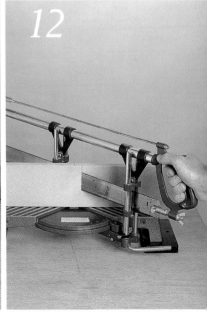

13 Clamp each plinth side in the workbench and use medium-grade abrasive paper wrapped around a sanding block to sand a bevel on the top front edge. How big you make the bevel is a matter of personal taste. Here, it was about 45 degrees. If you wish, draw lines on the top edge and front as guides.

14 Measure and mitre the plinth front to 785 mm (31 in), with the mitre facing in from the outer edge. Bevel the top as in step 13. Position the plinth pieces with a 25-mm (1-in) overhang at the bottom of the sides and front, drill and countersink three pilot holes for the front and two for the sides, apply glue and screw the plinth pieces in place.

15 Stand the settle upright and position the lid/seat-back assembly against the back. Mark, drill and countersink pilot holes through the seat-back to fix it to the back and sides. Make guide holes through the pilot holes, then apply glue and drive in screws.

16 Use a filling knife to push wood filler into the screw holes, leaving it protruding above the surface. Allow to dry completely and sand smooth. Dust off the settle and cover it with matt or gloss household paint.

Helpful hints

You can sand a small bevel on the top front and side edges of the opening lid, but make sure this is the same depth along the whole front and sides.

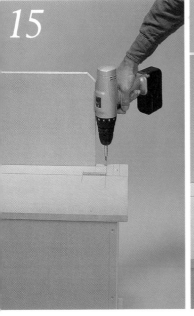

making a **bookcase**

This bookcase is designed to be constructed with the minimum of fuss – none of the screws used is driven in through the front or sides, thus cutting down the time needed for preparation before painting. The shelves are part of the carcase and don't just rest on the supports. Where you position them will depend on the size of books (or photographs, ornaments and so on) you intend to keep in the bookcase.

Materials (all timber is MDF unless otherwise stated)

2 pieces 1370 x 19 x 305 mm (54 x ¾ x 12 in) •
4 pieces 405 x 19 x 230 mm (16 x ¾ x 9 in) •
1 piece 1370 x 19 x 405 mm (54 x ¾ x 16 in) •
8 pieces softwood 230 x 25 x 25 mm (9 x 1 x 1 in) •
4 pieces softwood 405 x 13 x 63 mm (16 x ½ x 2½ in) •
38-mm (1½-in)-no. 6 screws

Tools

Crosscut saw or jigsaw • Combination square • Straightedge •
Bradawl • Pencil • Drill with pilot hole and countersink bits •
Screwdriver • Medium-grade
abrasive paper and
sanding block •
Masking tape •
PVA glue

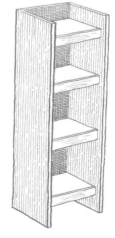

Skill level

Intermediate

Time

3–4 hours

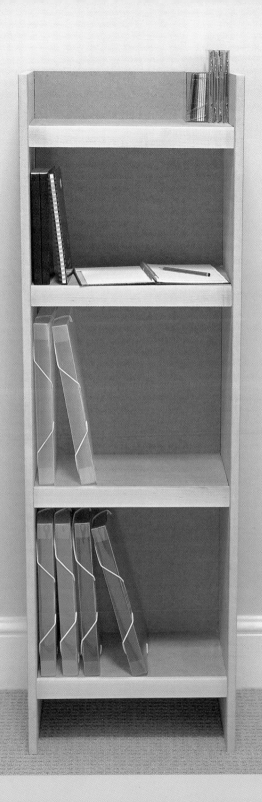

1   Measure and cut the four shelves to 405 x 230 mm (16 x 9 in) from 19-mm (¾-in) MDF. In this project the shelves are an integral part of the carcase, so it is essential they are cut square. To help you cut accurately, clamp a straight piece of thick timber to the cutting line to guide your crosscut saw.

2   Check the shelves with a square after cutting, and make sure all four pieces are identical. Make any adjustments, then butt a strip of 13 x 50 mm (½-x 2 in) softwood up to the front edge of each shelf and mark the shelf length exactly.

Helpful hints

You can cut or sand a slight bevel on the front edges of the shelf supports; measure 25 mm (1 in) back from the front edge along the lower side, draw diagonal lines to this on the sides and cut the bevel.

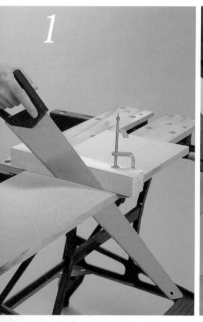

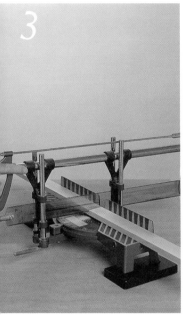
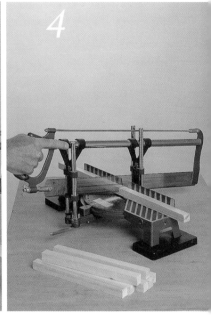

3 Set a mitre saw to 90 degrees and cut the shelf fronts. If you have cut them accurately, they should be identical as well as fitting exactly to the shelves' long edges. Check that the shelf front ends are square and sand them smooth.

4 The eight shelf supports are 230 mm (9 in) long, the same length as the shelf sides. Mark this measurement on a strip of 25 x 25 mm (1 x 1 in) softwood. With the mitre saw still set to 90 degrees, cut the shelf supports. Check that they are an accurate match to the shelf sides, then sand the ends smooth.

5 Each shelf support is glued and screwed to one side and a shelf, using two screws for each joint. To make sure the screws don't collide, butt the eight supports together using a square and mark a line 38 mm (1½ in) from each end. Centre the screw holes on these lines. Turn the supports onto the adjacent edge and mark lines and screw holes 19 mm (¾ in) inside the first holes. Drill and countersink all the holes.

6 Cut the two sides to 1370 x 305 mm (54 x 12 in) from 19-mm (¾-in) MDF. Butt the sides together at their back edges and mark a line for the back 19 mm (¾ in) inside the back edges of the sides. Using a square and straightedge, mark the position of the support bottom edges along both sides. The bottom ones should be 100 mm (4 in) from the base, the middle two 355 mm (14 in) above each top edge, and the top ones 255 mm (10 in) above the last top edge.

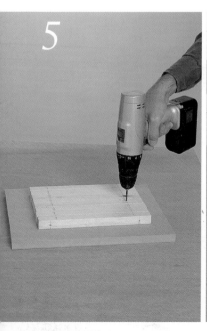
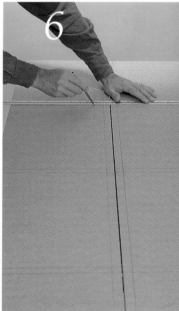

7 The shelf supports are screwed to the sides through the inner pair of pilot holes drilled in step 5. Position each support with one end butting up to the line for the back. Use a bradawl to mark the screw positions in the sides, apply glue to the meeting edge and drive in 38-mm (1½-in) no. 6 screws.

8 Cut the back to 1370 x 405 mm (54 x 16 in) from 19-mm (¾-in) MDF. Lay it flat and butt the sides up so the back fits in the drawn lines. Place the shelves in position on the supports, check the assembled carcase for squareness, then apply glue and screw the shelves onto the supports from below using 38-mm (1½-in) no. 6 screws.

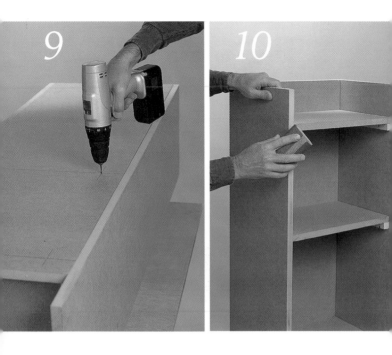

9 Check for squareness again and allow the carcase to dry completely. Mark the shelf positions on the back. Remove the carcase, lay it on its front and fit the back in place with the marked lines on the outside. Drill and countersink three pilot holes for each shelf with the outer ones 50 mm (2 in) in from the edges, then insert and drive in 38-mm (1½-in) no. 6 screws.

10 Stand the assembled bookcase upright and sand all the edges smooth with medium-grade abrasive paper wrapped around a cork or plastic sanding block. If you decide to sand a tiny bevel on the edges, make sure this is identical on each edge, otherwise the result will look sloppy.

11 Lay the bookcase on its back and apply glue to the front edges of the shelves. On this sort of length, regular dabs of glue are better than one thin, long line.

12 Place the shelf fronts in position and hold them there with masking tape, taking time to get the placing exactly right and pressing the tape firmly once you are satisfied. Allow to dry thoroughly, then apply primer to the softwood and paint in your chosen colour.

Helpful hints

The shelf fronts are glued on because they are purely decorative and should not suffer rough treatment. If you prefer, you can reinforce the glue by hammering and centre-punching small nails, then filling and sanding the holes.

making a
window seat

The lid of this window seat fits into place and is also removable, giving you extra storage space as well as a place to read or look out the window. The seat here was made to fit a recess measuring 770 mm (30⅜ in) long by 216 mm (8⅝ in) deep – you can adapt the dimensions to suit the requirements of your own window space.

Materials (all timber is softwood unless otherwise stated)

1 piece 652 x 38 x 38 mm (25¼ x 1½ x 1½ in) • 2 pieces 190 x 38 x 38 mm (7½ x 1½ x 1½ in) • 2 pieces 445 x 38 x 38 mm (17½ x 1½ x 1½ in) • 2 pieces 75 x 38 x 38 mm (3 x 1½ x 1½ in) • 2 pieces 912 x 38 x 38 mm (35⅞ x 1½ x 1½ in) • 2 pieces 415 x 38 x 38 mm (16⅜ x 1½ x 1½ in) • 2 pieces 106 x 38 x 38 mm (4¼ x 1½ x 1½ in) • 1 piece 405 x 19 x 38 mm (16 x ¾ x 1½ in) • 2 pieces MDF 476 x 19 x 143 mm (18¾ x ¾ x 5⅝ in) • 1 piece MDF 950 x 19 x 476 mm (37⅜ x ¾ x 18¾ in) • 1 piece MDF 950 x 19 x 402 mm (37⅜ x ¾ x 15⅞ in) • 63-mm (2½-in) no. 6 screws • 38-mm (1½-in) no. 6 screws

Tools

Jigsaw • Crosscut saw • Tenon saw • Sliding bevel • Spirit level • Combination square • Screwdriver • Drill with pilot and countersink bits • Straightedge • Pencil • Bradawl • Abrasive paper and cork or foam block • PVA glue • Wood filler

Skill level

Advanced

Time

4–5 hours

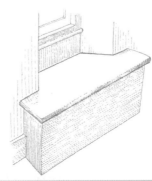

Simple home improvements

1 Measure up the back wall of the recess to the required height – here, 476 mm (18¾ in) – and use a spirit level to mark a line along the back and the recess sides. Place the body of a sliding bevel along the line at one of the recess corners, set the blade to the angle, and lock in this position.

2 Transfer the set angle from the sliding bevel to a piece of 38 x 38 mm (1½ x 1½ in) softwood, leaving enough at the end for a saw cut, then cut the angle. Mark whether it is the right or left side before repeating steps 1 and 2 at the other corner of the recess.

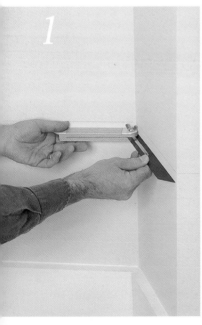

3 Mark and drill three pilot holes in the back batten, then countersink them. Hold the batten in position and mark through onto the wall, then drill the wall and fit the appropriate wall anchors. Position the batten and drive in 63-mm (2½-in) no. 6 screws.

4 Use the sliding bevel to fix the interior angles for the two recess side battens, then mark and cut pieces of of 38 x 38 mm (1½ x 1½ in) softwood to fit. Hold each batten in place, overhanging the side wall. Set the sliding bevel to mark the batten flush with the wall, then cut, drill and fix to the recess walls.

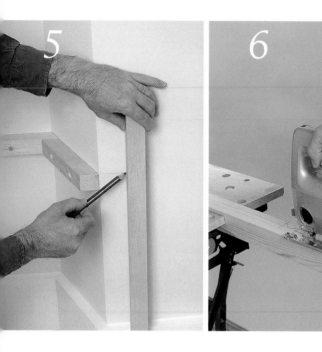

5 Use the spirit level to mark a line the same height as in the recess along the side walls. Hold a piece of 38 x 38 mm (1½ x 1½ in) softwood vertical to this line and mark the line. Then make another mark on the wood 38 mm (1½ in) below the first one. At the bottom, mark the height and depth of the skirting board onto the wood.

6 Clamp and cut the vertical batten to the shorter marked length, then reposition and reclamp it. Use a jigsaw or crosscut saw and tenon saw to cut the recess for the skirting board. Place in position, check for fit, and adjust as required. When satisfied, mark the position with a spirit level and fix to the wall as in step 3. Repeat for the other side.

7 With both vertical wall battens in place, lay a long piece of 38 x 38 mm (1½ x 1½ in) softwood across them, and mark the exact length of the top and bottom front frame members – here, 912 mm (35⅞ in). Cut both pieces to length.

8 The depth of the seat carcase will partly depend upon the depth of your recess, and the length of the two floor plates will be variable. Here, 305 mm (12 in) was suitable for the carcase, and the two floor plates were 75 mm (3 in). Place the floor plates in position, check for square, then drill, countersink and screw in place.

Helpful hints

When screwing together two or more butted pieces of wood, remember to mark them out so the screws do not meet each other in the wood.

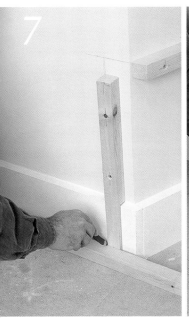

9 Lay the bottom frame member against the floor plates. Place a piece of 38 x 38 mm (1½ x 1½ in) softwood vertically on the end, and measure up to meet the line on the wall drawn in step 5, using a spirit level. Repeat on the other side, cut the vertical frame pieces to length, and drill and screw the four frame members together to make a rectangle.

10 Place the frame in position and measure from its inside edges to the wall; this should be the length of the floor plate plus the depth of the skirting board – here, 106 mm (4¼ in). Cut two side horizontal pieces from 38 x 38 mm (1½ x 1½ in) softwood, drill and screw them to the vertical wall battens. Then drill and screw the frame in place against the vertical battens and the floor plates.

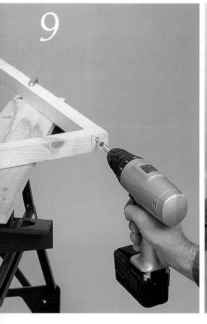

11 For the carcase sides, measure the outside of the side-frame assembly, including the recess for the skirting board. Transfer to 19-mm (¾-in) MDF, cut and fix to the sides as in step 5, this time using 38-mm (1½-in) no. 6 screws. Repeat for the front, but including the depth of the MDF sides already in place.

12 For the dimensions of the lid, measure across the sides, adding 19 mm (¾ in) on each side for the lid overhang, and the depth from the back of the recess to the front edge, again adding 19 mm (¾ in) for the overhang. Transfer to a piece of MDF and cut to size. Place this against the walls on the carcase and use a square to draw lines from the recess/outer wall corners across the lid.

13 Measure the depth of the carcase along these lines and mark them at this point. Mark the recess inner corners across the lid with a square and straightedge. Then mark the diagonal between the two sets of points. Shade in the waste, and cut the lid to shape.

14 Smooth the front and side edges of the top to a curve. You can use medium-grade abrasive paper wrapped around a sanding block, as here, or a power router and shaped bit. The end result should not cut into or scrape the legs of someone sitting on the seat.

Helpful hints

If you don't want a plain finish, consider adding some mitred moulding as a rectangle on the front. Or, mitre, fit and paint the skirting board to match the rest of the room.

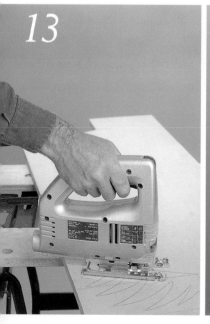

15 Place the top in position on the carcase and draw a line from beneath to mark the meeting point of the top and front. Make the line the full length of the front. Remove the top and lay it top-down, then draw a parallel line 19 mm (¾ in) in from the front one to show the depth of the MDF, and a further line 38 mm (1½ in) for the depth of the frame.

16 Measure and cut a lid batten from 19 x 38 mm (¾ x 1½ in) softwood – the one here is 405 mm (16 in) long. Mark, drill and countersink pilot holes, lay the batten with its outer edge against the innermost of the three lines, mark through the holes, and drive 38-mm (1½-in) no. 6 screws to hold it in place. Sand and paint the whole seat and lid to finish.

making an accessory stand

With its crisp, modern lines, this accessory stand could be used anywhere in the house for storing magazines, bathroom accessories, fruits and vegetables in baskets and so on. No joints are used in its construction – the skill comes in laying out and marking the pieces with accuracy, and in cutting mitres with precision.

Materials (all timber is softwood unless otherwise stated)

4 pieces 766 x 32 x 32 mm (30¼ x 1¼ x 1¼ in) •
4 pieces 485 x 19 x 19 mm (19 x ¾ x ¾ in) •
6 pieces 542 x 19 x 70 mm (21¼ x ¾ x 2¾ in) •
6 pieces 523 x 19 x 70 mm (20½ x ¾ x 2¾ in) •
10 pieces 505 x 19 x 19 mm (19¾ x ¾ x ¾ in) •
1 piece MDF 505 x 19 x 19 mm (19¾ x ¾ x ¾in) •
38-mm (1½-in) no. 6 screws • 32-mm (1¼-in) no. 6 screws •
25-mm (1-in) brad nails

Tools

Crosscut saw or jigsaw • Mitre saw • Combination square •
Straightedge • Bradawl • Pencil • Drill with pilot hole and
countersink bits • Screwdriver • Abrasive paper and sanding
block • Centre punch •
Hammer •
PVA glue •
Wood filler

Skill level
Intermediate

Time
3–4 hours

1 Measure and cut the four legs to 766 mm (30¼ in) from 32 x 32 mm (1¼ x 1¼ in) softwood. Check that they are all identical, then sand the ends smooth. Butt all four together exactly and use a combination square to mark two pairs of lines 19 mm (¾ in) apart, with the first top line 280 mm (11 in) from the top edge of the legs, and the second top line 280 mm (11 in) from the first bottom line.

2 Measure and cut the four slat supports to 485 mm (19 in) from 19 x 19 mm (¾ x ¾ in) softwood. Check that they are identical, sand the ends smooth, then lay them out as in step 1. Mark across the top edges for the positions of the five 19-mm (¾-in) slats – the outer ones starting 38 mm (1¼ in) from the ends, and the others with their centres at 125-mm (5-in) intervals from the outer ones.

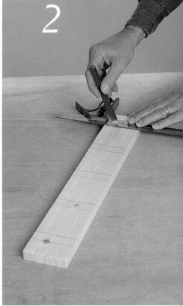

3 Lay the slat supports with the marked faces adjacent to the work surface. Draw lines 32 mm (1¼ in) in from each end on the uppermost faces, then mark, drill and countersink pilot holes through them.

4 Test-assemble one pair of legs with one pair of slat supports in position across the marked lines on the legs. Check for square, then apply glue to the meeting edges and drive in 38-mm (1½-in) no. 6 screws. Repeat for the other pairs of legs and slat supports, clean off excess glue and allow to dry.

5 Measure and cut the ten slats to 505 mm (19¾ in) from 19 x 19 mm (¾ x ¾ in) softwood, and check and sand as before. Place the pairs of legs on their sides. Clamp two scrap pieces below the slat supports to hold them and apply glue. Position the slats on the supports' top edges and drive in 32-mm (1¼-in) no. 6 screws through the outer pilot holes.

6 Repeat for all the outer slats until you have constructed a rectangular frame. Check for square, then glue and position each of the other slats, making sure the ends are exactly level, and drive in the screws. Allow the glue to dry.

7 Set the mitre saw to 45 degrees. Fit a length of
19 x 70 mm (¾ x 2¾ in) softwood into the mitre saw
with about 50 mm (2 in) over at one end. Cut the
wood and smooth the cut end with abrasive paper.

8 Hold the wood to the marks on the legs with the
mitred end protruding 19 mm (¾ in) past one leg. Mark
exactly where the other end meets a leg, then place
the wood in the mitre saw and cut, remembering the
mark is the inside of the 45-degree angle. Mark this
piece as a side or front/back rail.

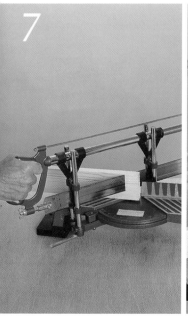

9 Continue to mark and cut the four lower rails – the sides should be 523 mm (20½ in) and the front/backs 542 mm (21¼ in). Lay the frame on its side, position each rail, then mark and drive in 25-mm (1-in) brad nails with a hammer. Make sure the nails are in line and equidistant for a neat finish.

10 Cut the top to 505 x 485 mm (19¾ x 19 in) from 19-mm (¾-in) MDF. Sand the sides smooth and check that they are square. Use a square and straightedge to mark lines 32 mm (1¼ in) inside each edge. At the corners make diagonals inside the drawn squares, then drill and countersink pilot holes through the meeting point. Screw the top to the top of the legs using 38-mm (1½-in) no. 6 screws.

11 Mark lines 25 mm (1 in) from the top of the legs for the lower edge of the four top front/back and side rails. Cut and fit these rails to meet the lines drawn and the top edge as shown in steps 7 to 9.

12 Finish by using a centre punch to drive all the nail holes below the wood surface. Fill these and the screw holes with wood filler and allow to dry. Sand the filler smooth, then apply wood primer and a top coat of your colour choice.

Helpful hints

To ensure that brad nails don't split the wood surface, either use a tiny drill bit to make pilot holes beforehand, or snip the sharp ends off the nails and then hammer them in.

chapter 2
Shelving

1. Fitting an alcove shelf

2. Making a hall shelf

3. Making a shelf with coat rail

fitting an alcove shelf

Fitting a shelf into an alcove is a popular way of making the most of space that would otherwise go to waste. The measurements given here are for a small-to-medium-size alcove, and you can obviously adapt them to suit your own requirements. The result is a sturdy piece of work that can take a surprising amount of weight – but don't push your luck by overloading it!

Materials (all timber is softwood)

1 piece 1145 x 19 x 200 mm (45 x ¾ x 8 in) •
2 pieces 1145 x 25 x 50 mm (45 x 1 x 2 in) •
2 pieces 145 x 25 x 50 mm (5¾ x 1 x 2 in) •
63-mm (2½-in) no. 8 screws • Wall plugs or anchors

Tools

Tenon saw • Crosscut saw • Sliding bevel • Spirit level •
Square • Screwdriver • Drill with 6-mm (¼-in), pilot and
countersink bits • Straightedge • Pencil • Bradawl • Abrasive
paper and cork or foam block • PVA glue • Wood filler

Skill level

Intermediate

Time

1–2 hours

Simple home improvements

1 Decide on the height of your shelf, then use a spirit
level and pencil to mark the bottom edge of the shelf –
that is, 19 mm (¾ in) below where you want the shelf
top to be – along the back wall. Extend this line across
the whole wall, then match this line along the alcove
sides to the length of your shelf minus 32 mm (1¼ in).

2 To measure the exact length along the back wall, place
the end of your measuring tape at one end and extend
the tape. When you reach the other end, position the
tape casing exactly in the corner and lock the tape.
Make a mark at the visible end of the tape, take this
dimension, and add the length of the tape casing,
embossed along it.

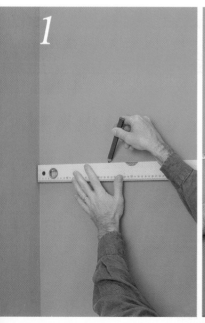

3 Cut a strip of 25 x 50 mm (1 x 2 in) softwood to length
– here, 1145 mm (45 in) – then sand the ends square.
With its top edge positioned along the line in the
alcove, check that it is an exact fit. Drill pilot holes
every 255–305 mm (10–12 in) along this back support
and countersink the holes.

4 Hold the back support exactly in position on the back
wall again. Use a bradawl to make a mark for the wall
plugs or anchors through each screw hole. Draw a
cross for each, with the meeting point of the lines
exactly over the bradawl marks.

Helpful hints

When measuring an alcove, never assume that the length at
the back wall is the same as at the alcove front. Always
measure and check both lengths.

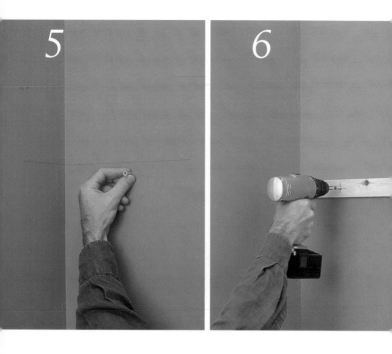

Fit a 6-mm (¼-in) bit into the power drill, then drill through the wall at each cross mark. Insert wall plugs or plasterboard anchors, tapping them into place gently with a rubber mallet if necessary.

Place the back support into position on the wall, insert 63-mm (2½-in) no. 8 screws into each holes, and tighten them.

Helpful hints

You don't have to paint the shelf and its supports the same colour – use any colour combination you wish. Here, the supports were painted the same colour as the wall.

7 Cut the side supports to the length of the line on the alcove sides – here, this is 145 mm (5¾ in), the width of the shelf less 32 mm (1¼ in). Drill and countersink two pilot holes in each support, then fix to the alcove sides as for steps 4–6. It is essential that the top edges of each of the supports are on an identical level.

8 Use a sliding bevel to check whether the front support will be the same length as the back one. Set the bevel to 90 degrees and place it into each corner; a gap will tell you if there is a discrepancy. Set the bevel to the angle of one corner.

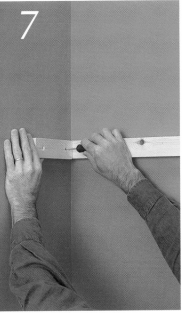

9 Transfer the bevel angle to the wood for the shelf, drawing it within the end of the piece to make cutting accurate. Mark the shelf back the length of the back support, then take the angle of the other corner and transfer it to the shelf at the mark, then cut. Sand smooth the ends.

10 Place the shelf in position on the supports and mark on the underside the front edges of the side supports. Remove the shelf and draw a line across the underside between the marks. Cut the front support to the exact length along this line.

11 Continue the line along the sides and top of the shelf, then drill and countersink three or four pilot holes for the front support. Place the front support in position, bradawl through the pilot holes, apply glue, and screw into place.

12 Reposition the front shelf on the supports. Mark, drill and countersink pilot holes through the front support into the front edge of the side supports, then apply glue and screw into place. Fill all screw holes with wood filler, allow to dry, and sand smooth. Apply primer and a top coat of paint.

Helpful hints

To make less work for yourself, you can buy ready-made wooden shelves from most DIY shops. These usually have shaped or moulded front edges.

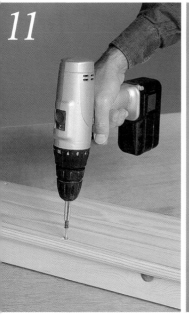

making a **hall shelf**

This simple hall shelf uses a basic housing joint to hold the back in place. These joints are all about accurate marking and cutting – the ideal situation occurs when you are only using glue and screws to reinforce a good, tight fit. To gain confidence using a power jigsaw, draw patterns and profiles on sheets of waste timber, MDF or plywood, and practise your control and accuracy on them.

Materials (all timber is softwood)

1 piece 815 x 25 x 178 mm (32 x 1 x 7 in) • 2 pieces 305 x 25 x 140 mm (12 x 1 x 5½ in) • 1 piece 760 x 25 x 178 mm (30 x 1 x 7 in) • 38-mm (1½-in) no. 6 screws • 38-mm (1½-in)-brad nails • 2 brass coat hangers and screws

Tools

Crosscut saw • Tenon saw • Straightedge • Combination square • Jigsaw • Screwdriver • Drill with pilot hole and countersink bits • Hammer • Abrasive paper and cork or foam block • PVA glue • Wood filler

Skill level

Beginner

Time

1–2 hours

1 Measure and cut the pieces to size from 25-mm (1-in) softwood. The two uprights are 305 x 140 mm (12 x 5½ in), the top is 815 x 178 mm (32 x 7 in) and the back 760 x 178 mm (30 x 7 in). Check the corners are square on all pieces, and sand the ends smooth with abrasive paper wrapped around a sanding block.

2 Place the two uprights exactly together along their sides. Pin them together and drive in brad nails to hold them. Transfer the profile to one of the sides, and shade in the waste wood to be cut out.

Helpful hints

You can get inspiration for profiles on the uprights by looking at old furniture, or from books on folk-art patterns and profiles. Remember, however, the aim of the game is strength.

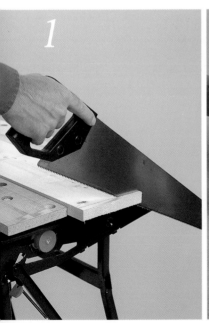

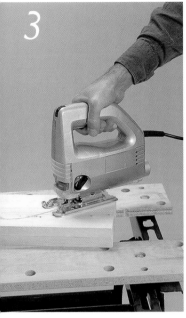 

3 Clamp the uprights on a bench or work surface, and use a jigsaw to cut out the profile. Position the jigsaw guide just on the waste side of the pattern line, and move the jigsaw smoothly. With the uprights still clamped, use the abrasive paper and block to get a smooth, identical shape.

4 Remove the uprights from the clamp. To draw the housing joint, lay flat one upright and place the end of the back piece against one side corner. Carefully draw around the edge of the back.

5 Repeat step 4 for the other upright, making sure you position the back on the appropriate corner. Shade in the waste wood, then clamp as before and cut out the housing joints with a crosscut saw or jigsaw.

6 Measure 13 mm (½ in) along the sides and front from the corners on the top. Draw a diagonal between the end marks and cut the mitres off. Then sand down the rough edges using abrasive paper wrapped around the cork block.

Helpful hints

To fit the shelf to a wall, drill and countersink two screw holes in the back of it before painting. Hold the shelf to the wall, check that it is level and mark the screw holes. Drill the wall, insert wall plugs or anchors, and screw in the shelf.

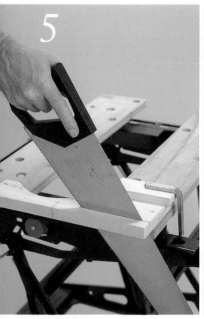

7 Fit the back panel into place in the housing joints in the uprights. Make any adjustments for a close fit, check for square, then hold in place and drill and countersink three equidistant pilot holes through the back into the uprights. Apply glue to the meeting edges, and insert and tighten 38-mm (1½-in) no. 6 screws.

8 Place the top in position, and drill and countersink two equidistant pilot holes through into the uprights. Drill two more holes into the back panel, then disassemble, apply glue, insert and tighten the screws. Fill all the screw and nail holes with wood filler, and sand smooth when dry before painting.

making a
shelf with coat rail

The principle behind this project is the same as for the hall shelf on page 64; the difference is that for this one you need to make up wall plates to hold a metal coat rail. The dimensions here are for an alcove 1158 mm (45½ in) wide and 510 mm (20 in) deep; you can adapt the cutting sizes to suit your own requirements.

Materials (all timber is MDF unless otherwise stated)

2 pieces 355 x 19 x 150 mm (14 x ¾ x 6 in) •
1 piece softwood 1120 x 25 x 75 mm (44 x 1 x 3 in) •
1 piece 1158 x 19 x 190 mm (45½ x ¾ x 7½ in) •
Coat rail 1120 x 19 mm diameter (44 in. x ¾ in diameter)
plus ends and screws • 38-mm (1½-in) no. 6 screws •
Wall plugs or anchors

Tools

Crosscut saw or jigsaw • Combination square • Sliding bevel •
Straightedge • Bradawl • Pencil • Drill with pilot hole and
countersink bits • Screwdriver • Abrasive paper and
sanding block • Spirit level • PVA glue • Wood filler

Skill level

Intermediate

Time

2 hours

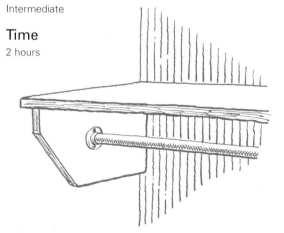

Simple home improvements

1 Mark a line for the top of the wall plates and batten along the side and back walls of the alcove, using a spirit level on each wall. Make sure this is accurate.

2 Cut the two wall plates to 355 x 150 mm (14 x 6 in) from 19-mm (¾-in) MDF. To match the width of the batten, draw a line 75 mm (3 in) from the top edge across the length of each plate. Set the combination square to 45 degrees and mark an angle to the bottom edge from this line. Shade the waste.

Helpful hints

Always check the angle of the alcove side walls to the back one; it may look a perfect right angle, but assuming that it is without checking can ruin a project.

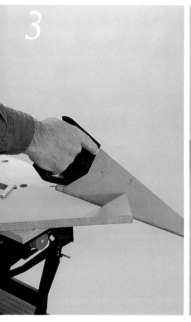
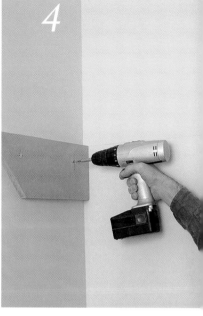

3 Clamp one wall batten to the workbench and use a
crosscut saw or jigsaw to cut off the waste MDF.
Smooth the cut edges with abrasive paper wrapped
round a block, then repeat for the other wall plate.

4 Drill and countersink two pilot holes about 75 mm
(3 in) from the ends along the line. Hold the wall plate
in position, mark the wall through the holes, then
remove the plate. Drill the wall, and insert wall plugs
or anchors. Position the plate again and screw into
place. Repeat on the other side wall.

5 Measure between the wall plates at the back – here, the length was 1120 mm (44 in). Cut a piece of 25 x 75 mm (1 x 3 in) softwood to length and sand smooth the ends. Drill and countersink three pilot holes at equidistant intervals. Then hold the batten in position and mark the wall holes. Drill and fit plugs in the wall as before and screw the batten in place.

6 Mark on the wall plates for the rail ends, remembering to allow for lifting coat hangers above the rail. Measure between the wall plates for the length of the rail. Stretch the tape measure across, and when the tape and the casing fit perfectly, lock the tape and add the length of the casing to that shown on the tape.

7 Transfer the measurement to the metal rail – here, the 1158-mm (45½-in) alcove, less the two 19-mm (¾-in) wall plates, gave a length of 1120 mm (44 in). Clamp the rail securely and cut it accurately with a hacksaw. Smooth off the cut edges and hold in position with the ends in place, bradawl the screw holes in the plates and drive in the screws.

8 Measure across the back wall of the alcove for the back of the shelf. Hold the sliding bevel to get the angle of the side wall, lock the bevel and transfer the angle to 19 x 190 mm (¾ x 7½ in) MDF. Repeat on the other wall, then cut the shelf. Sand smooth the ends, position on the batten and wall plates, drill and countersink pilot holes, then glue and screw the shelf in place.

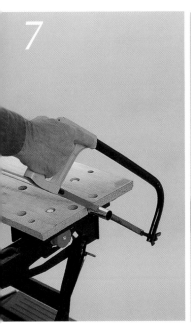

chapter 3
Closets

1. Making a shoe rack

2. Making a wardrobe with loose cover

3. Fitting an alcove storage unit

4. Fitting louvre doors

making a **shoe rack**

On floors or in closets, shoes and boots have a way of expanding to fill the space available, so this rack should provide a tidy answer to the problem. The construction is quite straightforward, but the real skill lies in the measuring and marking out. Take your time and be prepared to check everything more than just once.

Materials (all timber is MDF unless otherwise stated)

2 pieces 815 x 19 x 330 mm (32 x ¾ x 13 in) •
1 piece 815 x 19 x 510 mm (32 x ¾ x 20 in) •
1 piece 510 x 19 x 75 mm (20 x ¾ x 3 in) • 12 pieces
softwood 510 x 25 x 25 mm (20 x 1 x 1 in) • 38-mm (1½-in)
no. 6 screws • 38-mm (1½-in) brad nails

Tools

Jigsaw or crosscut saw • Mitre saw • Combination square •
Screwdriver • Drill with pilot and countersink bits •
Straightedge • Pencil • Bradawl • Hammer • Abrasive paper
and sanding block • PVA glue • Wood filler

Skill level

Intermediate

Time

2–3 hours

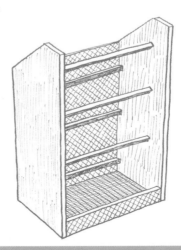

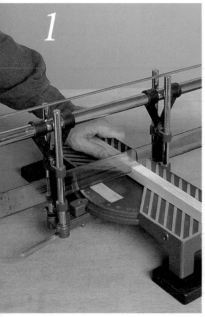

1 Set the mitre saw to 90 degrees and mark and cut twelve pieces of 25 x 25 mm (1 x 1 in) softwood to 510 mm (20 in). This is where a mitre saw is particularly useful, because the sawn ends will be all but square.

2 Even with the mitre saw, you must check the ends for square. Lay flat a few pieces at a time, and butt them up to a flat surface, then use the combination square to check that they are identical in length and square. Sand the ends. For the back, mark and cut a piece of 19-mm (¾-in) MDF to 815 x 510 mm (32 x 20 in).

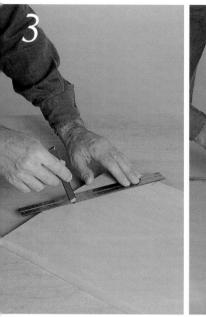

3 Mark and cut the MDF for the front kick to
510 x 75 mm (20 x 3 in). Cut the two MDF sides to
815 x 330 mm (32 x 13 in), then mark out the top
mitres. Join a line starting 100 mm (4 in) from the back
edge and the same down the front. Shade in the
waste, cut both mitres, and check that they are
identical before sanding all the MDF pieces smooth.

4 Lay the sides down with their back edges together
and their top and bottom edges meeting exactly. Mark
a line 19 mm (¾ in) inside from the meeting edge
lengthwise along both pieces. From these lines, mark
across the sides for the positions of the back rails: the
bottom one 50 mm (2 in) from the bottom, then the
middle one 255 mm (10 in) above that and the top one
a further 255 mm (10 in).

5 The lines across the sides represent the top edges of the back rails. Stand a rail on end with its top edge meeting the line and its back edge against the length-wise line, then mark round the rail. Draw diagonals between the corners for the pilot hole centre, then repeat for all the rails on both sides.

6 From the lengthwise lines, measure 200 mm (8 in) along the horizontal lines and mark at this point. Use a square to measure up 100 mm (4 in), and mark this for the top point of each front rail.

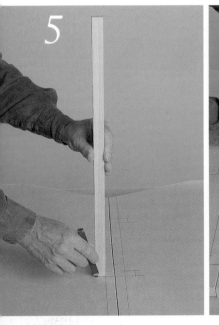

7 Draw a line from the top back edge of each top rail to the top points of each front rail. Position each front rail along this angle with the top point meeting the mark, then draw around each rail as in step 5.

8 Fit a small bit in a power drill, and drill pilot holes at each diagonal centre, working from the inside out. Clean off the waste on this side. Turn the sides over, then fit a countersink bit into the power drill and countersink the holes from the outside.

Helpful hints

Drilling pilot and guide holes is often thought of as a minor part of a project, but badly centred ones can mar the look of a piece as well as lessening the strength. Hold the drill square to the workpiece and apply pressure smoothly.

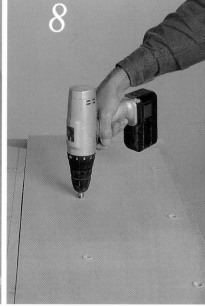

9 Lay down the back and sides with their inside edges butted up exactly to the back. Using a square and straightedge, mark lines across the back between the bottom back rail lines on the sides. This must be an exact fit, or the rack will not sit together well.

10 Apply glue to the back rails, position them on the lines across the back, then hammer in 38–mm (1½-in) brad nails every 10–150 mm (4–6 in) along the rails. Clean up any excess glue before it dries completely.

Helpful hints

You can keep shoe-cleaning materials, spare shoelaces, shoe trees and so on in the space behind the front kick and beneath the bottom rails.

11 Hold each side up square to the back with the side back edges flush to its rear edge, then mark, drill and countersink pilot holes every 200–255 mm (8–10 in). Apply glue, insert 38-mm (1½-in) no. 6 screws, and tighten them.

12 Use a bradawl through the back rail pilot holes, then apply glue, insert the screws and tighten them. Hold each front rail in position, then repeat this process. Place the front kick in position, then mark for pilot holes and fit as in step 11. When the glue is dry, sand the whole piece and paint it.

making a **wardrobe with loose cover**

If you don't have a wardrobe or alcove space, a free-standing clothes rack is a great way to hang your clothes. Designed for a single rack, this wardrobe incorporates a simple, easily assembled frame and a six-piece cover.

Materials (all timber is softwood unless otherwise stated)

4 pieces 1525 x 32 x 32 mm (60 x 1¼ x 1¼ in) •
4 pieces 720 x 32 x 32 mm (28⅜ x 1¼ x 1¼ in) •
4 pieces 495 x 32 x 32 mm (19⅜ x 1¼ x 1¼ in) •
8 pieces plywood 195 x 3 x 160 mm (7¾ x ⅛ x 6¼ in) •
4 pieces plywood 150 x 3 x 125 mm (6 x ⅛ x 5 in) •
25-mm (1-in) no. 6 screws • 1 piece chambray denim
1575 x 828 mm (62 x 32½ in) • 1 piece chambray denim
828 x 592 mm (32½ x 23¼ in) • 2 pieces chambray denim
1575 x 592 mm (62 x 23¼ in) • 2 pieces chambray denim
1575 x 485 mm (62 x 19 in) • 2 pieces chambray denim
915 x 75 mm (36 x 3 in)

Tools

Crosscut saw or jigsaw • Combination square • Straightedge

• Bradawl • Pencil • Drill with pilot hole and countersink bits • Screwdriver • Abrasive paper and sanding block • Scissors • Pins • Needles • Basting and sewing threads • Tailors' chalk • Yardstick • Sewing machine

Skill level

Intermediate

Time

4–5 hours

Simple home improvements

1 Cut the four frame uprights to 1525 mm (60 in), the four front and back rails to 720 mm (28⅜ in), and the four side rails to 495 mm (19⅜ in), from 32 x 32 mm (1¼ x 1¼ in) softwood. Check that each set of four pieces is identical in length, and sand the ends. Lay two upright and two side rails together to make a rectangle, check for square, then drill and countersink pilot screw holes. Drive in 25-mm (1-in) no. 6 screws.

2 Repeat for the other upright and side pieces. Mark, drill and countersink pilot holes for the front and back rails in both rectangular assemblies, making sure the holes do not crash into the screws already in place. Hold each rail in position, check with a square, then push a bradawl through the pilot hole before driving in the screw. Repeat for all the rails until you have a square-corner frame.

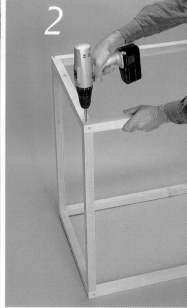

3 Mark out four 230-mm (9-in) squares and two 185-mm (7¼-in) squares on a sheet of 3-mm (⅛-in) plywood, then mark one diagonal across each square. Clamp to the workbench and cut out the squares with a fine-tooth crosscut saw. Saw across the diagonals on each square to make two triangles.

4 Use a square to mark cutting lines from the square edges of the triangles – the eight triangles for the sides should be 195 x 156 mm (7¾ x 6¼ in), and the four for the back 150 x 125 mm (6 x 5 in). Cut to size, then hold each one in turn in position, just inside the edges of the frame, then drill and countersink pilot holes and screw in place.

5 All the pieces of fabric can be cut from a single 1220-mm- (48-in)-wide piece 6.4 m (7 yd) long. Lay out the fabric and use tailors' chalk to mark the back to 1575 x 828 mm (62 x 32½ in), the top to 828 x 592 mm (32½ x 23¼ in), the two sides to 1575 x 592 mm (62 x 23¼ in), the two front pieces to 1575 x 485 mm (62 x 19 in) and the two ties to 915 x 75 mm (36 x 3 in).

6 Cut out all the pieces with scissors, making sure you cut accurately along the chalk lines. It's a good idea to pin the pairs of pieces together with a paper label so you don't get confused later.

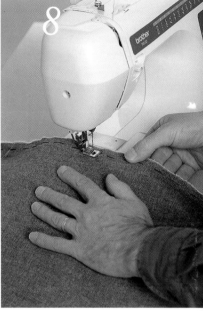

7 Pin one long edge of each side piece of denim to the corresponding length of the back, and pin the top to the back in the same way. Baste the joins using thread of a contrasting colour.

8 Sew the joins together using matching thread on a sewing machine. The seam allowance for all the joins should be 13 mm (½ in). Turn the joined pieces inside out to check that your seam is straight. This is the procedure for all seams throughout this project.

Helpful hints

As well as pinning two pieces of fabric along the edges that will be basted and sewn, insert a few pins elsewhere in the body of the fabric to ensure that it does not slide or move out of position.

9 Turn the front edge of the top back 6 mm (¼ in) and sew this flat using a zigzag stitch. Repeat for the long front edges of the side pieces. Pin the sides to the top, baste as before, then stitch in place.

10 Fold one long tie in half along its length. Sew across one end then along the length, leaving the other end open. Turn the tie inside out and press it flat, then hand-stitch the opening. Repeat for the other tie.

Helpful hints

It's vital that you fit brand-new needles in your sewing machine before starting a new project, especially when using a heavy fabric like chambray denim. Check that they're the right size, too.

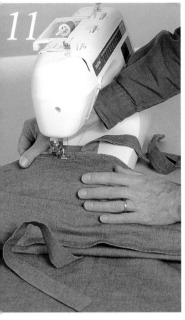

Position one front piece against one side and place the middle of one tie across the seam line on the outside. Pin and baste this front seam to join the front, side and tie, then sew the three pieces together. Repeat for the other side.

Tuck the top edges of the front under, then pin and baste them before sewing with a zigzag stitch to a neat, flat finish. Place the cover over the frame, then pin up the hem all around at the bottom. Remove the cover, press the hem flat and stitch it.

fitting an alcove
storage unit

If storage space is tight, being able to use all the space in your home becomes a priority. Alcoves so often are just filled with clutter, but some thought and imagination can transform them into efficient and attractive storage modules. The dimensions here are for an alcove 1145 mm (45 in) wide and over 510 mm (20 in) deep. A word of warning about the chest of drawers: don't use anything that is valuable or may become so, one day!

Materials (all timber is MDF unless otherwise stated)

1 piece 1145 x 19 x 430 mm (45 x ¾ x 17 in) •
1 piece 1835 x 19 x 430 mm (72 x ¾ x 17 in) •
2 pieces 430 x 19 x 400 mm (17 x ¾ x 15¾ in) •
1 piece 405 x 19 x 150 mm (16 x ¾ x 6 in) •
5 pieces softwood 405 x 19 x 25 mm (16 x ¾ x 1 in) •
Hanging rail 635 x 19 mm diameter (25 x ¾ in diameter) •
38-mm (1½-in) no. 6 screws • Chest of drawers 800 x
460 x 466 mm (31½ x 18 x 18¼ in) • Wall plugs or anchors

Tools

Crosscut saw or jigsaw • Mitre saw • Hacksaw •
Combination square • Straightedge • Pencil • Spirit level •
Drill with pilot hole and countersink bits • Screwdriver •
Abrasive paper and sanding block • Bradawl • Adhesive tape

Skill level

Intermediate

Time

4–5 hours

1 Place the chest of drawers against one side wall of the alcove and check that it is square with a spirit level; you may have to add wedges to straighten it. Cut one piece of 19 x 430 mm (¾ x 17 in) MDF to the required height – here, 1830 mm (72 in) – and stand it square against the chest side. Check with the level, then mark the height and draw a line along the back wall.

2 Remove the upright and use the spirit level to mark a line along the alcove side walls. To find the front edges of the top piece, mark a line vertically from the front of the chest along the side wall, and join this to the horizontal line.

3 Measure the distance for the top batten along the chest-side wall – this should be about 25 mm (1 in) less than the depth of the top. Mark and cut a piece of 19 x 25 mm (¾ x 1 in) softwood, and bevel the under-side of the front edge with a mitre saw set to 45 degrees. Next, drill and countersink pilot holes, and screw to the wall using wall plugs or anchors.

4 Measure across the alcove and cut the top to size – here, 1145 x 430 mm (45 x 17 in) – from 19-mm (¾-in) MDF. Replace the upright against the chest and check for square, then lay the top in place, resting across the upright and on the batten. Check with the spirit level, then mark a line for the bottom edge on the other side wall.

5 Remove the top and upright. Measure and cut the wall plate from 19 mm (¾ in) MDF, again 25 mm (1 in) or so short of the top and wide enough to take the hanging rail – here, 405 x 150 mm (16 x 6 in). Drill, countersink and fix to the wall as for the opposite side.

6 Measure and cut four more battens, adding a bevel to the front edge as before. Drill, countersink and fix two to the wall as in step 3. Replace the upright and use a spirit level to mark across to the upright.

Helpful hints

If your chest of drawers is not very heavy, remove the bottom drawer, drill through the back and fix this to the skirting board behind with screws.

7 Stand the upright against the back wall and draw lines for the inner battens along the upright, using a square and straightedge. Drill, countersink and fix the battens to the upright using 38-mm (1½-in) no. 6 screws.

8 Place the upright in position against the chest again, check for square and get an assistant to hold it exactly in position while you drill through the upright into the chest side, countersink, insert and tighten screws. For stability, it's best to position the screws at the top and bottom of the chest.

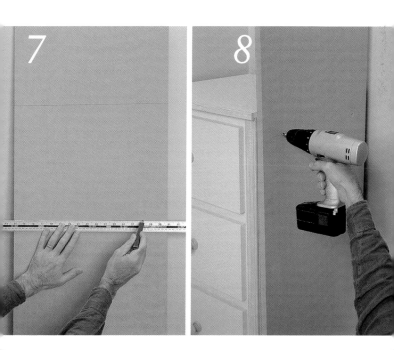

9 Replace the top, then measure and mark the batten, wall plate and upright edges from below. Remove the top and use the lines to mark, drill and countersink pilot holes. Replace the top in position, then insert and tighten screws.

10 Measure across between the wall and the upright for the shelves, then cut to size from 19 mm (¾ in) MDF – here, they were 400 mm (15¾ in) long and the same width as the upright. Place each in turn on its battens, and plane or sand as necessary for a close fit. The shelves in this project are free-standing and removable. If you want to fix them to the battens, do this before screwing on the top, and work from the bottom one upward.

11 Measure the length for the hanging rail across the tall unit, and cut the rail with a hacksaw. Tape the fittings on the rail ends, hold the rail up to the desired height and mark the screw holes on the wall plate. Mark on the upright, using a spirit level to ensure straightness.

12 Bradawl the screw holes in the wall plate and upright, then use the screws supplied with the hanging rail hardware to fix it in place. Remove the rail and fixings before sanding and painting the unit, then replace when the paint is completely dry.

Helpful hints

The height of the shelves above the chest of drawers will depend entirely on what you want to use them to store. If in doubt, make them equal distances between the chest top and the unit top.

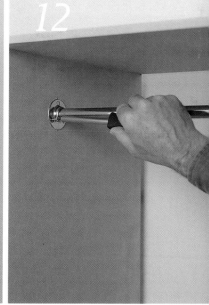

fitting **louvre doors**

Ready-made louvre doors are available in set heights and widths from many DIY and timber stores. They are a good way to create an attractive closet front for an alcove, as shown in this project, or you can use them to replace plain-front old closet doors anywhere in the house. Make sure you fit them with the louvres facing down.

Materials (all timber is softwood)

2 pieces 2140 x 50 x 50 mm (84 x 2 x 2 in) •
1 piece 1078 x 25 x 50 mm (42½ x 1 x 2 in) •
1 piece 150 x 19 x 50 mm (6 x ¾ x 2 in) •
1 piece 2140 x 25 x 100 mm (84 x 1 x 4 in) •
1 piece 610 x 25 x 100 mm (24 x 1 x 4 in) •
1 piece 1145 x 25 x 200 mm (45 x 1 x 8 in) •
38-mm (1½-in) no. 6 screws • 63-mm (2½-in) no. 6 screws •
2 louvre doors • 6 brass 50-mm (2-in) flush hinges •
2 wood handles • 2 magnetic door catches

Tools

Crosscut saw or jigsaw • Combination square • Straightedge •
Bradawl • Pencil • Drill with pilot hole and countersink bits •
Screwdriver •
Abrasive paper
and sanding block

Skill level

Intermediate

Time

3–4 hours

Simple home improvements

1   Measure out from the back wall of the alcove or
closet along both side walls. If you already have
shelving or units in place (see pages 56 and 94), allow
a little room in front of them; otherwise, make sure
you have enough space for the wall battens to be
fitted comfortably into the alcove.

2   Use a spirit level to mark a line for the outer edge of
the wall batten on one alcove wall, then extend the
line to the full height of the batten. Because not every
alcove has right-angle corners, use a square from this
first line to draw across the front of the alcove, thus
ensuring that the battens will be square to each other.
Mark for the other batten.

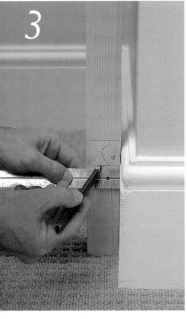

3 Cut the wall battens to length from 50 x 50 mm (2 x 2 in) timber – here, 2140 mm (84 in) – then stand one upright to its marked line on the wall (an assistant can do this). Check it with a spirit level. Use a square to mark the height and depth of the skirting board on the batten, then mark any curved profiles. You can mark the skirting board shape onto a template.

4 If you used a template, transfer the profile onto the bottom of the batten. Clamp the batten to the work-bench and use a jigsaw to cut the profile. Remove the batten and check it against the skirting board, making adjustments to the profile until it fits' snugly in place. Repeat steps 3 and 4 for the other batten

5 Drill and countersink pilot holes through each batten. Hold each one in place, and mark through the holes onto the wall. Drill and insert wall plugs or anchors. Screw the battens in place using 63-mm (2½-in) no. 6 screws.

6 Measure and cut the floor plate to fit between the skirting boards of the alcove walls from 25 x 50 mm (1 x 2 in) wood – here, it was 1078 mm (42½ in). Drill and countersink pilot holes to fit to the front of the battens, making sure they don't meet any holes through the battens into the wall. Screw into place using 38-mm (1½-in) no. 6 screws.

Helpful hints

If you don't have an assistant to hold the doors for you, use wedges to keep them at the right height when measuring and fitting.

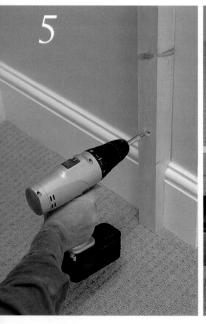

7 Cut the back wall plate to 150 mm (6 in) from 19 x 50 mm (¾ x 2 in) wood, and drill and countersink pilot holes. Mark the back wall with a line the same height as the battens, then centre the plate and fix as for the battens. Cut the front upright to the same length as the wall battens from 25 x 100 mm (1 x 4 in) wood, and the horizontal front-to-back piece, to fit to the alcove back wall, from the same lumber. Screw them together, checking at each stage for squareness.

8 Centre the front upright and horizontal piece across the floor plate and resting on the wall plate. Check with a spirit level, then drill and countersink pilot holes through the front and into the wall plate from above. Drive in 38-mm (1½-in) no. 6 screws.

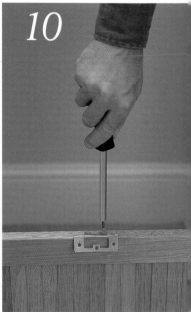

9 Ask an assistant to hold each door in place. Make a mark 3 mm (⅛ in) above the top on each wall batten, allowing a small gap at the bottom for opening and closing. Cut the frame top piece to the width of the alcove – here, 1145 mm (45 in) – from 25 x 200 mm (1 x 8 in) wood. Fit this to the marks, mark, drill and countersink pilot holes, then screw in.

10 For doors of the height used here, you will need three 50-mm (2-in) brass flush hinges per side – shorter doors can use two. Allow a minimum distance of 100 mm (4 in) from the top and bottom for the outside hinges, and position the third one equidistant between the others. Make pilot holes with a bradawl and screw the hinges in place.

11 Get an assistant to hold a door in place to a wall batten, with enough allowance so the door can open and close smoothly. Position the hinges against the batten and bradawl pilot holes for the hinge screws. Drive in the screws firmly, checking that the door functions properly. Repeat for the other door.

12 Mark the positions of the magnetic catches on the frame upright and inside faces of the doors with a bradawl. Screw on the catches, making sure they allow the doors to lie flat against the upright. Fit the handles to the doors.

Helpful hints

For a lasting finish on the doors, use one or more coats of clear matt varnish. After filling and sanding the screw holes, paint the frame to match the colour of the wall.

glossary

Batten – a narrow strip of wood; often used to describe such a strip used as a support for other pieces

Bevel – any angle other than a right angle at which two surfaces meet

Butt joint – a simple joint where two pieces of wood meet with no interlocking parts cut in them

Countersink – to cut, usually drill, a hole that allows the head of a screw, nail or pin to lie below the surface

Crossbar – moulded wood separating glass panes

Galvanized – screw or nails covered with a protective layer of zinc; used mainly for exterior work

Housing – a shallow, wide groove cut across the grain of a piece of wood; housing joints are where a piece of wood is fitted into a housing

MDF – medium-density fibreboard; a prefabricated material that can be worked like wood

Mitre – a joint made by cutting equal angles, usually at 45 degrees to form a right angle in two pieces of wood; cutting such a joint

Pilot hole – a small-diameter hole drilled into wood to act as a guide for a screw thread

Rail – a horizontal piece of framing in a door or window

Rebate – a stepped, usually rectangular, recess cut along the edge of a piece of wood as part of a joint

Ripping – sawing wood along the grain

Softwood – wood cut from trees, like pine, maple and cedar, belonging to the botanical group *Gymnospermae*

Stile – a vertical piece of framing in a door or window

Template – a cut-out pattern on paper or cardboard, used to help shape wood

Upright – a vertical piece of wood used in making a frame or carcase

index

accessory stand **46–53**
    finishing **53**
    front/back rails **51–2, 53**
    legs **48–9**
    materials and tools **46**
    slats **50**
    slat supports **48–9**
    top **52**
alcove shelf **56–63**
    back support **59**
    fitting **62–3**
    materials and tools **56**
    measuring the alcove
        58–9
    painting **60, 63**
    side supports **61**
alcove storage unit **94–101**
    battens **98**
    chest of drawers **94, 96,**
        98
    hanging rail **101**
    materials and tools **94**
    shelves **100–1**
    top **97, 100**
    upright **96, 99**
    wallplate **98**

bookcase **28–35**
    assembly **34–5**
    back **33–4**
    finishing **34**
    materials and tools **28**
    shelf fronts **31, 35**
    shelves **30–2**
    sides **32**
brad nails **53**
butt joints **41**

casters **17**
closets
    loose cover wardrobe
        86–93
    shoe rack **78–85**

doors, *see louvre doors*
dust mask **12**

fibreboard, cutting **12**

hall settle **18–27**
    cutting parts **20–1**
    fitting base **22**
    fitting sides **22**
    hinges **24–5**
    lid/seat back **23–4, 27**
    materials and tools **18**
    plinth **25–6**
hall shelf
    back panel **66, 69**
    finishing **69**
    fitting to wall **68**
    housing joints **67–8**
    materials and tools **64**
    uprights **66–7**
hinges **24–5, 108**
housing joints **67–8**

jigsaw **12, 64, 66–7, 105**

louvre doors **102–9**
    catches **109**
    finishes **109**
    frame **106–8**
    hanging **106, 109**
    hinges **108**

materials and tools **102**
wall battens **104–5**

MDF (medium density fibreboard) dust **12**
mitre joints **51**
mitre saw **51, 80**

pilot holes **53, 83**
profiles **12, 64, 66–7, 105**

settle, *see hall settle*
shelf with coat rail **70–5**
back batten **74**
cutting and fitting shelf **75**
materials and tools **70**
metal rail **74–5**
wall plates **72–3, 73**
shelving
alcove **56–63**
with coat rail **70–5**
hall **64–9**
ready–made **63**
shoe rack **78–85**
back **80**
cutting rails **80**
fitting rails **83–5**
front kick **81**

materials and tools **78**
sides **81–2, 85**
sliding bevel **38–9, 61**

toy box **10–17**
assembly **15–16**
base **14, 16**
casters **17**
cutting parts **12–13**
lid **13, 15**
materials and tools **10**
painting **10, 17**

wardrobe, loose–covered
86–93
cutting the fabric **90**
making the frame **88–9**
materials and tools **86**
sewing the fabric **91–3**
window seat **36–45**
depth **41**
finishes **44–5**
frame **41–2**
lid **43–4, 45**
materials and tools **36**
sides **43**
use of sliding bevel **38–9**
wall battens **38–40**

acknowledgements

All photographs taken by Alistair Hughes, except for:

8/9 Camera Press; 54/55 Lucinda Symons/ Robert Harding
Syndication; 76/77 Rowland Roques-O'Neil/ Robert Harding
Syndication

Illustrations by Stewart Walton.